Wrong Number, Right Connection

A Guide to Phone Sex with:

Bill Collectors

Telemarketers

Customer Service

Wrong Numbers

Misdialed Calls

Written by Clark Henny

Table of Contents

Introduction.. 4

Chapter 1 6

Chapter 2 9

Chapter 3 12

Chapter 4 14

Chapter 5 17

Chapter 6 19

Chapter 7 21

Chapter 8 22

Chapter 9 24

Chapter 10..27

Conclusion 29

Introduction

Growing up, I never could have imagined how a chance encounter with risqué TV commercials would introduce me to the alluring world of phone sex. It was 1978, and I had just moved to New York City, eager to pursue a career in stand-up comedy. I worked as a host at a nearby restaurant to make ends meet. After late-night performances, I'd often return home, flip on my tiny TV, and channel-surf, including a local New York cable channel that caught my eye.

The channel featured seductive women speaking in sultry tones, beckoning viewers to call them. Though I knew they were likely actresses, I was drawn to the fantasy. The idea was tempting - you'd get to speak with the gorgeous woman from the commercial, who'd say, in her sexiest voice, "Call me. I'm waiting for you." It was the ultimate escapism, especially given the era's limited access to explicit content.

These phone sex operators were skilled artisans adept at crafting verbal fantasies that transported callers to new realms of pleasure. With their sultry accents, seductive singing, and erotic tones, they knew how to keep men on the line. Their goal was simple: keep the caller engaged for as long as possible, racking up the bill, all while maintaining the illusion of intimacy. It was a delicate balancing act, one that required finesse and creativity.

As alluring as these services were, they came with a hefty price tag. Calls could quickly add up to a couple of hundred dollars an hour, leaving callers with a staggering bill. The unspoken rule was that operators would prolong the caller's pleasure, teasing them with sensual fantasies while racking up the minutes. For those who could afford it, the experience was undoubtedly exhilarating. However, for someone like me, living on a tight budget, it was nothing more than a pipe dream.

As I navigated this frustrating period, I was torn between desire and financial reality. The siren's call of phone sex operators was tantalizing yet utterly out of reach. With no affordable alternatives for accessing explicit content, I felt like I was stuck between a rock and a hard place. It was a difficult time, and I couldn't help but wonder what the future held.

Chapter 1

Dialing Up Desire

The idea for this book came to me unexpectedly, sparked by a surprising discovery. I found myself becoming aroused while listening to a woman's voice on the phone, even when our conversation was completely non-sexual. Her tone, pitch, and subtle nuances triggered my strong physical response.

At first, I kept this to myself, unsure how the women I was talking to would react. However, as I continued to experience this phenomenon, I realized that I didn't need explicit content or participation from the other person to achieve arousal. This discovery was both surprising and liberating.

I no longer felt the need to pay for phone sex services or try to convince someone to engage in explicit conversations with me. Instead, I could enjoy the sound of a woman's voice and let my imagination run wild.

I recall one particular experience that stood out. I was on the phone with a woman discussing everyday topics like the weather, her family, and her daily activities. But what caught my attention wasn't the content of our conversation; it was her tone of voice and breathing. Those subtle cues triggered a moment of intense excitement within me and got me very hard.

What I found fascinating was that our conversations were not explicit or sexual. Yet, I was able to reach a state of arousal without needing explicit content. This realization was both surprising and intriguing.

This experience also taught me the importance of discretion. Since we weren't on a video call, I was able to keep my reactions private. This got me thinking about applying this concept to other areas of my life beyond just romantic or social interactions.

I began to wonder: what if I could experience this same level of arousal and intimacy with women in other contexts? What if I could dial up desire with someone as mundane as a bill collector, telemarketer, customer service representative, or even a wrong number?

The possibilities seemed endless, and I became excited to explore this concept further. And so, the idea for this book was born – a journey to explore the intersection of intimacy, arousal, and connection in the most unexpected way with unexpected callers.

Chapter 2

Healthy Phone Sex

Phone sex in loving relationships can indeed be a healthy, exciting, and intimate way for couples to connect and explore each other's fantasies. By engaging in personal and meaningful conversations, partners can strengthen their bond, rekindle passions, and maintain closeness despite physical distance.

The benefits of phone sex in loving relationships include:

- **Increased intimacy**: Phone sex allows couples to engage in intimate conversations, sharing their desires, fantasies, and feelings.

- **Improved communication**: Phone sex encourages open and honest communication, helping partners to understand each other's needs and desires better.
- **Enhanced creativity**: Phone sex can be a fun and creative way for couples to explore new fantasies and scenarios together.
- **Increased excitement**: The thrill of sneaking around to have a hidden conversation can be exhilarating and add to the excitement of phone sex.

To make the most of phone sex in a loving relationship, consider the following tips:

- **Be spontaneous**: Surprise your partner with a naughty wake-up call or a sultry goodnight conversation.
- **Get creative**: Experiment with different scenarios, fantasies, and role-playing to keep things exciting and fresh.
- **Communicate openly**: Communicate your desires, boundaries, and feelings with your partner to ensure a positive and enjoyable experience.
- **Have fun**: Most importantly, remember to have fun and enjoy the experience with your partner!

Phone sex is a complex and multifaceted phenomenon that can be viewed from various angles. Here are some additional perspectives:

1. **Emotional Intimacy**: Phone sex can foster emotional intimacy by allowing partners to share their desires, fantasies, and feelings in a private and comfortable setting.
2. **Trust and Vulnerability**: Engaging in phone sex requires trust and vulnerability, as partners must feel secure sharing their intimate thoughts and desires with each other.
3. **Creativity and Imagination**: Phone sex encourages creativity and imagination, as partners must rely on verbal cues and their imagination to create a shared experience.
4. **Convenience and Accessibility**: Phone sex can be a convenient and accessible way for partners to connect intimately, especially for those with busy schedules or physical limitations.
5. **Exploration and Discovery**: Phone sex can provide an opportunity for partners to explore new desires, fantasies, and boundaries in a safe and controlled environment.
6. **Communication and Feedback:** Phone sex requires effective communication and feedback, which can help partners better understand each other's needs and desires.

By considering these diverse perspectives, we can gain a deeper understanding of the complexities and benefits of phone sex in intimate relationships.

But this book is NOT about phone sex with your loving partner.... It's anything butt that!

Chapter 3

Dealing with Debt Collectors

Throughout my life, I've faced financial challenges due to circumstances like divorce and economic downturns. Debt collectors frequently contacted me when I struggled to pay bills on time. Their calls were often persistent and impersonal.

Initially, I responded defensively but realized this approach wasn't productive. So, I tried a different strategy. When interacting with debt collectors, I used humor to diffuse tension. I'd make lighthearted comments unrelated to the topic.

This approach often caught them off guard, and they'd typically ignore my remarks and continue with their script. I found this method amusing and helpful in coping with the stress of dealing with debt collectors.

Here are some examples of lighthearted sex comments I've made during calls:

1. "You have a great voice! It's really getting me hot and bothered."
2. "I love your accent! It's getting me really hard."
3. "I'm glad we could have this conversation. You're helping me understand my situation while I am touching myself."
4. "I appreciate your patience. You're making this process much easier for me. I am so close to cumming."
5. "Is it okay if I ask, are you having a good day so far, and how wet are you?"
6. "I really want to stick my tongue down your thirsty throat."

Using humor and sexual comments, I've found that I could make difficult conversations more enjoyable and less stressful.

Chapter 4

Wrong Number, Right Affair

Years ago, I received a wrong number call that unexpectedly turned into a phone sex encounter. The caller was looking for someone else, and I decided to play along, adopting the identity of the person she was trying to reach.

As the conversation progressed, it became clear that the person she was expecting was someone she was romantically involved with. Despite feeling uneasy, I continued with the charade. The caller assumed I was the person she sought, and the conversation became increasingly intimate.

Looking back, I didn't feel guilty, as I wasn't scamming or cheating her out of money. She had mistaken me for someone else, and I decided to play along.

Phone Foreplay

Since then, I've found that wrong numbers can be a fun opportunity to showcase my sexual improv skills. It's interesting to see where the conversation goes and how far I can take it.

In other cases, people would call looking for someone else, and I'd let them know they had the wrong number. Sometimes, I'd use my persuasive skills to keep them on the phone, and we'd have an interesting conversation.

Reinforcing the idea that it may be fate that they dialed my number; there's no such thing as mistakes. These conversations took an unexpected turn a few times, and we'd end up having a more personal and intimate conversation.

The callers would often be surprised by how the conversation went and how they felt afterward. Some exhibited a strange sense of guilt as if they felt like they were cheating. But can you really be unfaithful when having phone sex with the wrong number?

Connecting with someone over the phone can be challenging, especially when the number is wrong. The key is to keep the person on the line and establish a connection. This can be achieved by using humor, being friendly, and showing genuine interest in getting to know them.

Once a connection is made, it's possible to build an engaging, enjoyable conversation that can turn sexual. However, it's essential to respect the other person's boundaries and comfort level...that is if you are not hung up on ...

Chapter 5

Spam Calls and Telemarketers: Turning Frustration into Entertainment

Spam calls can be annoying and disruptive, often involving automated messages or scams. As someone who's received their fair share of these calls, I've learned to recognize and entertain myself with them.

One memorable experience was with a suspicious caller who threatened me and demanded personal information. I decided to have some fun, providing fake details accompanied by over-the-top reactions. The caller continued threatening me, but I kept up the act, turning the conversation into a humorous and explicit exchange.

Another amusing encounter was with a telemarketer trying to sell me insurance. Each time they attempted to make a sale, I steered the conversation toward intimate topics, sharing graphic details and responding to their quotes with provocative remarks.

While these interactions can be entertaining, it's essential to remember that spam calls can be vicious, aiming to emotionally upset and panicked recipients. It's crucial to stay vigilant and protect personal information.

Turning spam calls into entertaining experiences is a way for me to regain control and have a good laugh.

Chapter 6

The Unconventional Art of Phone Sex

The Unconventional Art of Phone Sex with Customer Service Representatives

As someone who's experienced the challenges of phone sex with customer service representatives, I can attest that it's often frustrating due to language barriers. Many representatives, typically from India, struggle to understand nuances and subtle cues.

It's only recommended if you find humor in miscommunication. However, I've discovered that befriending representatives, making them laugh, and playful teasing can lead to unexpected outcomes.

As a former corporate trainer for a Fortune 500 company, I understand the rigorous training representatives undergo. My approach is to engage with finesse, as highly trained representatives pick up on everything.

While my goal isn't always phone sex, I've managed to secure dates with representatives. Although they didn't lead to meaningful relationships, it's impressive that I've turned customer service calls into romantic encounters.

On rare occasions, I've successfully turned a customer service call into phone sex. One notable instance involved keeping a woman laughing for almost an hour, using humor as foreplay.

While successes are exceptions rather than the rule, it's clear that unconventional connections can be made with customer service representatives.

Chapter 7

Right Connection

"One of the most astonishing phone sex encounters involved my friend and a woman I had met a couple of nights prior. We had spent 11 hours talking at a coffee shop, and I was smitten. However, while I was out of town a few days later, she called me, and my roommate answered the phone. He recorded the call, which was inappropriate. What I heard was unbelievable - he had turned a casual conversation into an explicit and intense phone sex call. I was shocked, as this was a completely different side of her. After hearing that call, I never pursued a relationship with her."

Chapter 8

Setting the Mood for Intimate Phone Conversations

To elevate your intimate phone experiences, consider having these essentials within reach:

1. Personal care items: A good lubricant, tissues, and wipes for comfort and hygiene.
2. A washcloth for tidiness and cleanliness.
3. A private, quiet space to minimize distractions and interruptions.
4. Soft, sensual background music to create a relaxing ambiance.

5. A hands-free phone or speaker for convenience and freedom.
6. A comfortable seating arrangement, such as a plush bed or chair.
7. A refreshing beverage to stay hydrated and focused.
8. Loose, comfortable clothing to promote relaxation and intimacy.

Timing is also crucial. Intimate conversations may be more enjoyable during quieter, more relaxed hours, such as late evening or nighttime.

Ensure a clear and stable phone connection to minimize interruptions. By considering these essentials and factors, you can create an atmosphere conducive to meaningful and enjoyable intimate phone conversations.

Chapter 9

Does and Don'ts of Phone Sex

When engaging in phone sex, there are key strategies to keep in mind to create a thrilling and intimate experience.

Present Tense is Key

Always speak in the present tense to create a sense of immediacy and intimacy. Instead of saying "I wish" or "when I see you," say "I'm doing this to you now."

Embracing Imagination

When a woman expresses hesitation, emphasize the power of imagination. Respond with something like:

"Imagination is the sexiest thing a man or woman can have. For example, when you watch a movie or TV show, you know it's not real, but you get involved. Let's use our imagination to create a thrilling experience."

Guiding the Conversation

Guide the conversation and keep the focus on the fantasy. When she tries to deflect or express uncertainty, use phrases like:

- "Turn your brain off, sweetheart. Just relax and let me guide you."
- "You don't need to know me. Trust me and allow yourself the pleasure of my seduction."
- "I know you don't know me, but that makes this exciting. You're stepping out of your comfort zone."

Embracing the Thrill

If she expresses surprise at her own behavior, respond with:

"That's what makes it amazing. It's your first time, and it's exciting."

If she says, "I don't know why I'm doing this. This is crazy," reply with:

"The craziest moments in life are often the most fun. Let's enjoy this thrill together."

Chapter 10

From Boredom to Ecstasy. First Date Phone Calls.

After years of navigating the dating scene, I was stuck in a cycle of unfulfilling phone calls. Conversations felt more like job interviews, with women asking generic questions like "Where do you live?" "What do you do for work?" and "What's your favorite color?" These well-intentioned inquiries left me feeling drained and uninspired.

Determined to break the monotony, I decided to take a different approach. Since I had no intention of meeting these women in person, I decided to try to turn the calls into something more exciting. I'd respond to their mundane questions with provocative answers, hoping to ignite a spark.

Sometimes, the women were shocked by my responses, but I saw it as an opportunity to transform the conversation. I aimed to turn the call into something thrilling, even if it meant being a bit outrageous. When women engaged with my explicit comments, the conversation would shift from bland to bold, and we'd embark on a thrilling adventure together.

These encounters were short-lived but transformed tedious phone calls into something electrifying. While my approach might have been unorthodox, it added a spark to dull conversations...

Conclusion

The argument can certainly be made that engaging in sexual conversations with bill collectors - telemarketers - customer service - wrong numbers - and pre-first-date callers can be seen as inappropriate and disrespectful. Many bill collectors, customer service reps, and telemarketers are professionals performing their job duties, and they are not in a position to consent to sexual conversations. Such behavior can indeed be viewed as an abuse of power, a lack of empathy, and a disregard for others' boundaries. But over my lifetime, I have used this behavior as a coping mechanism for the stress and anxiety caused by overly zealous debt collection, annoying telemarketers, and obnoxious customer service reps. I am not preaching this behavior as a healthy or respectful way to manage stress. just my way of turning annoying - obnoxious- contentious - tedious calls into sexually charged communication many times resulting in orgasm.

It is crucial to prioritize respect, empathy, and consent in all interactions. Alternative, healthy coping mechanisms can be found for dealing with the stress of these types of calls.

I just haven't found any. Thus, this book….

Why did I write this book? It's not a grand, sweeping narrative like "War and Peace," nor a biblical epic. Some might even consider its themes a little unsettling. However, for me, it was a necessary exploration.

Over the years, I've received countless calls from telemarketers, spam callers, and bill collectors. These interactions often left me feeling annoyed and adversarial, ruining my day. Instead of engaging with them directly, I could take a more comedic, playful approach.

This method became my defense mechanism against these obnoxious calls. I've not harmed anyone by doing so, and I've even found it an enjoyable challenge. When I receive wrong numbers or misdialed calls, I try to turn them into humorous, flirtatious exchanges.

While I may not have started the call, it's fair game since they initiated the contact. Nowadays, with caller screening, I receive fewer spam calls.

Nonetheless, I still encounter dull, introductory phone calls as a single person navigating the dating world.

That's where my experience comes in handy. I've learned how to transform these mundane conversations into something more exciting. Phone sex can be a fun, creative way to connect with others, and I'm happy to share my expertise.

This book may not change the world, and I'm still determining how well it will be received. Nonetheless, I felt compelled to write it, reflecting my personal experiences. If my story makes you laugh, smile, or approach future phone calls with a different attitude, then I've accomplished my goal.

My book may make your subsequent encounters with bill collectors, telemarketers, wrong numbers, or customer service representatives less stressful and more enjoyable. That's my hope.

THE END

Made in the USA
Las Vegas, NV
15 December 2024

14418344R00018